The Unshakable Woman

The Unshakable Woman
4 Steps to Rebuilding Your Body, Mind and Life
After a Life Crisis

by Dr. Debi Silber

www.PBTInstitute.com

Praise for Dr. Debi Silber and *The Unshakable Woman*

"I work out 3 - 5 x a week, eat well, consider myself a soulfully and physically fit 58 year old female. After suffering a heart attack and needing 3 stents I was in psychological shock. This book is GREAT for anyone who is so caught up in the thick of their life and wants to finally make a change in their mind, body and soul. No nonsense, motivating, inspiring, short and to the point! If you are "ready" (to rebuild your life), get set because this book will take you where you want to go." – Kathy Ligouri

"Phenomenal information for ALL WOMEN on shifting from breakdown in your life to breakthrough. Thanks so much Debi for your brilliant work and support. The Unshakable Woman: 4 Steps to Rebuilding Your Body, Mind and Life After a Life Crisis." – Freddy Zental Weaver

"This little book has so much to offer. It's got just the right mix of inspiring story with practical advice and how-to. For those of us overworked and stressed out women, this is a God send. I hope Silber keeps writing and sharing her wisdom." - Light

"We all face crisis moments in our lives at one point or another, and can grow and get stronger as a result. Finding the resilience to face life's challenges can be tough, and Debi Silber's new book is a great resource! She provides practical strategies for finding the opportunities amidst the challenges, and leading an even better life as a result. As a clinician, I work with many parents whose lives have been turned upside down when they find out their child has special needs. This book is a great resource to help them navigate the emotions and challenges, and come out better as individuals and parents on the other side. I look forward to recommending this book to many parents at my clinic!" – Dr. Nicole Beurkens

"This book is incredible for helping you to rebuild your life and mind after any difficult obstacle. The Unshakable Woman will show you how to leverage any circumstance with grace and confidence. Thank you Debi for writing this book and sharing your process for becoming an unshakable woman!" - Alex

"This book is a must read whether you are a super soccer mom or a busy executive. The book has simple and easy strategies anyone can implement into their life to improve their health and mindset on every level. A must read!" – Joe Tatta

"Trauma and crisis is something many women struggle with in my practice. Debi Silber has written a beautiful and incredibly useful book to help us during those most difficult and overwhelming times. Highly recommend." –Alejandra Carrasco, M.D.

"This is a book that I highly recommend for anyone who is facing a crisis in their lives. Debi gives practical advice to rebuild and overcome difficult situations." – Jack

Printed in the United States of America
ISBN: 1543050840
ISBN: 978-1543050844

Debi Silber, 535 Broadhollow Road, Suite B12
Melville, New York 11747
Debi@PBTInstitute.com
www.PBTInstitute.com

OTHER BOOKS BY DR. DEBI SILBER

The Unshakable Woman: The Workbook (Silber; 2017)

A Pocket Full of Mojo: 365 Proven Strategies to Create Your Ultimate Body, Mind, Image, and Lifestyle (Silber; 2014) This book is recommended by Brian Tracy and Marshall Goldsmith.

Ordering Information:
Quantity sales. Special discounts are available on quantity purchases by corporations, associations, and others. For details, contact the publisher at the address above.

ACKNOWLEDGMENTS

A very special thank you to Adam, Dani, Dylan, Camryn, and Cole. I love you all, and you have each taught me many of my greatest lessons in life. Thank you to my incredible family and friends for your love and support. Thank you to Alissa Schwartz, Anna Miranda, Paul Saladino, and Guy, who all played a vital role in helping me heal from a life crisis that put me on a path far greater than I ever imagined. Thank you to my amazing clients, who continue to blow me away with their determination, resilience, and strength; to my team, who helps me share my message; to my mastermind and "growth" friends, who inspire me to dream big; to Stacey Canfield for the cover photo; to Karen Lacey and Jessica Vineyard for copyediting; and finally, a huge thanks to you. Yes, you, the person who trusted me enough with their time to invest in this book. I take that seriously, and it is my intention to deliver. I am filled with gratitude, thanks, and appreciation.

FOREWORD

Debi Silber is a woman after my own heart: strong, to-the-point, and full of the practical encouragement it takes to stay healthy in a crisis. She knows what it means to face hard times and come out unshaken, and that strength and compassion shows in her words and actions.

My own hardest time came in September 2012, when my teenage son was the victim of a horrific hit-and-run accident. In that single moment, I came face to face with my worst nightmare.

So I can testify firsthand that the words of wisdom in *The Unshakeable Woman* are exactly what someone in that position needs. Whether your own challenge comes in the shape of an illness, relationship loss, or financial crisis, the advice in this book will carry you forward from tragedy to healing.

None of us will escape this life trouble-free. But how you handle the hard times can shape not only your own future, but the lives of everyone around you. This short, powerful book is the perfect companion to ensure you meet your obstacles with grace, hope, and courage.

-JJ Virgin
Fitness and Nutrition Expert and
NY Times best-selling author of titles including The Virgin Diet, JJ Virgin's Sugar Impact Diet, and Miracle Mindset: You Are Stronger Than You Think

A FEW WORDS BEFORE WE GET STARTED

Does this sound like you? You have a lot on your plate, managing work, home, family, and possibly aging parents, too. In order to get things done, you have gotten used to putting yourself last, taking care of your needs if and when everyone else's needs are cared for.

Unfortunately, by that time, you have no time, energy, or motivation left for your own self-care.

Because you have so much on your plate, you have found some creative ways to cut a few corners. The first place is the easiest: your own self-care. Think about it. If you wake up a little bit earlier, you can send out a few more emails. If you give up a workout, you can get a few more errands done. If you go to the drive-thru, you don't have to take the extra time to make a healthy meal at home—you get the idea.

You are also exhausted. Saying no to others is hard, especially if you have been conditioned to be a people pleaser like many of us. So, while you desperately need some time for yourself, you keep saying yes to chores, tasks, responsibilities, and errands that pull you away from what is meaningful to you, leaving you to say no to things that make you happy.

Burning the candle at both ends but not taking the time you need to refuel or recharge, you have found an alternative fuel source too: sheer willpower and adrenaline, fueled by sugar and caffeine. Sure, it allows you to keep going, but you are doing everything in that "tired-and-wired-unsustainable-long-term-energy" kind of way.

Finally, you have discovered that you can save time by thinking instead of feeling. Feelings take time to process and slow you down, so you dim the part of yourself that feels, becoming almost machine-like as you turn up the doing and turn down the being.

In this process of surviving, it is likely that you are neglecting the parts of life that bring you joy and fulfillment, too. You feel numb, barely surviving as you sleepwalk through your day in an effort just to get through it. If you are in a relationship, you may have grown apart from your partner. If you have kids, you might be less patient with them. If you work, you may find that your job isn't bringing you the same sense of fulfillment it once did. You may also find that you mask an increasing amount of stress-related symptoms with medications, alcohol, sleeping aids, or antidepressants.

You do all you can to distract yourself from the areas of life that aren't working, because if you stop and take the time to look at them, you will remove the last pebble holding back the avalanche. Sure, you get it all done, but it is not without a price. You may feel exhausted, overwhelmed, overweight, unfit, unfulfilled, and unhappy.

Without some sort of change, this is the perfect scenario for a life crisis, and there are many kinds. It can be an illness, a tragedy, or a trauma that can shake up your world as you have known it and cause you to hit rock bottom. It could be a midlife crisis, where suddenly you start questioning what you are doing, how you have been living, and whether it is time to make some changes in order to live more deeply and fully. You might have that wake-up call from a traumatic experience, or you could become triggered by something you see happening around you or from an overwhelming emotion that starts to bubble up from within. You may ask yourself if it is time to pursue a passion or leave that dead-end job. You may wonder if it is time to find alternative ways to heal from an illness that conventional medicine hasn't been able to cure. You may gain the courage to pick up the pieces and start over after a broken relationship or decide to recreate the one you are in. Or you may be ready to listen to that wise inner voice that has been gently urging you to take that bold next step in a brave and new direction.

Sound familiar?

You are not alone. I get it, because I have been there. That was me as well as thousands of clients I have been blessed to work with over the last twenty-seven years. They felt broken, numb, depleted, exhausted, frustrated, and unhappy . . . just *done*.

From this broken and confusing place, how do you regroup and heal while still managing all of your responsibilities? How do you identify and decide what path to take when you have been on the same path for so long that you are almost entirely on autopilot? How do you gather the strength, resilience, and resolve to not just bounce back but to use this opportunity to heal physically, mentally, emotionally, psychologically, and spiritually so you become better than ever before?

I am so glad you are here, because from this frightening and unfamiliar place, you are going to create a lifestyle plan that has you looking, feeling, and living much better. You are going to have strategies to start rebuilding your body, your mind, and your life. I have been there. I have found a way to heal from more than a few major life crises (such as a dangerous infection that nearly took my life, the death of a loved one, chronic illness and disease, gut-wrenching heartbreak, massive betrayal, mental and emotional abuse, depression, and more), and I am going to teach you how you can use your illness, crisis, tragedy, or trauma as the catalyst to create and live a life you love. If you haven't had a life crisis that you consider severe, that will work, too. I will teach you the key questions to ask yourself in order to find out what you really want and what may be stopping you, along with ways over, around, and through those obstacles so you can start living a life that is filled with purpose, passion, and meaning. Sound good?

Here is how this book works. In working with countless women as well as healing from many challenges myself, I have found that what seems to help us the most lies within four major categories. Each of those categories are covered in Part 1, Part 2, Part 3, and Part 4 along with topics that fall within each category. The categories are in a specific order for a reason. They are strategically placed because I have found that my clients and I had the best results taking on certain principles at specific times. For example, while getting healthy is very important (Part 4), when you have just been traumatized by a life crisis, or if a midlife crisis is knocking on your door, monitoring your eating and exercise probably isn't what you want to put your attention on. You are reeling from your situation, feeling confused, and want to make sense of what happened. You want to find meaning in why things occurred as they did and get your head in the right place so you can get through your day and move forward. When your mental and emotional health improves and you have more clarity and direction, you are more willing to make the changes you need to create a lean, fit, healthy, and energetic body. Make sense?

Also, I know you are busy, so while I could dive deeply into each point, my intention is to give you what you need to get results. Besides being an action-oriented coach, a mom of four kids and six dogs, running a business, and recently finishing a PhD program for Transpersonal Psychology, I get the whole busy thing, so everything I teach comes from that place. I will be giving you the necessary information to make the changes you need to in order to look, feel, and live better. My greatest passion is to help women just like you become unshakable, and I hope you feel my support in every word throughout this book. So, with a virtual hug and my deepest respect for your willingness to heal and grow, let's get started.

Contents

FOREWORD BY JJ VIRGIN

A FEW WORDS BEFORE WE GET STARTED

Intoduction

PART 1: WILLINGNESS TO CHANGE AND GROW

Chapter 1. Help from Spirituality: How to Hear those Supernatural Secrets Whispering in Your Ear

Chapter 2. Forgiveness: Why It Is So Hard and How to Do It

Chapter 3. Death and Rebirth: Shedding the Old, Embracing the New

PART 2: MINDSET

Chapter 4: Change Your Thoughts, Change Your Life

Chapter 5. Building Beliefs by Building Bridges

Chapter 6. A Step-by-Step Process to Reveal the Ultimate Version of You

Chapter 7: Strengthening the Gatekeeper

PART 3: RELATIONSHIPS

Chapter 8: How to Climb Out of the Crab Bucket

Chapter 9: Romantic Relationships: What Do You Need Now?

PART 4: HEALTH

Chapter 10: How Stress Makes Us Sick, Fat, Old, and Exhausted—
And What to Do About It

Chapter 11: Nutrition: Creating a Lean, Healthy Body

Chapter 12: Fitness: A Strong Body Equals a Strong Mind—And
Looks Great, Too

Chapter 13: Living an Unshakable Life

Chapter 14: New Path and Next Steps

ABOUT THE AUTHOR

Introduction

Few of us go through life unscathed. It is how we handle those challenges makes us who we are. At some point in our lives, most of us will experience some type of life crisis. That crisis can be an illness, a tragedy, or a trauma of some kind. It can be the death of a loved one, losing the job that has been paying the bills, receiving a frightening diagnosis, or navigating a divorce and all it entails. It can be the trauma that emerges because of a betrayal from someone you trusted or what you must deal with after experiencing physical, mental, emotional, sexual, or verbal abuse. It can be a midlife crisis, where you suddenly realize you have been mindlessly letting time and opportunities pass you by and find yourself starting to question who you are, what you are doing, how you are living, and what you want.

Whatever your particular life crisis is, it gave you a wake-up call, a shift, or a full-blown psychological earthquake. It can be something mild or something so traumatic that your life becomes forever compartmentalized into two camps: "before it happened" and "after it happened." Just as an earthquake divides the Earth, a psychological earthquake divides us into who we were before the crisis and who we become as a result. Those traumas cause our foundation to be rocked, our worldview to be challenged, and our beliefs to be questioned and changed. They can cause a shift of such magnitude that it forces us to rethink and renegotiate everything we have known to be real and true. They can cause gut-wrenching pain, soul-crushing heartache, fear, intense anxiety, rage, sadness, confusion, anger, frustration, and despair.

While there are many negatives that result from these life-altering experiences, please keep an open mind to allow a new idea to marinate: some of these challenges can be exactly what we need. They can be the ultimate shake-up, the exact wake-up call and catalyst we need to wake us up and change in order to live the life we want most. Finally, they can create "post-traumatic growth," a phenomenon researched by Richard G. Tedeschi and Lawrence G. Calhoun, whose research has shown that while it appears that an emotionally painful event leaves only negative consequences, stress, and pain, the event can also create an incredible opportunity for healing and growth as the person being impacted by the trauma gains a new awareness, perspective, and wisdom they didn't have access to before the event occurred.

These traumas totally disrupt and dismantle our world. We become completely and powerfully overwhelmed from these painful experiences as they take us down and under from a blow we believe we may never heal from. How we emerge from the struggle can give us a glimpse at how this painful and life-altering experience can lead us to enormous growth. From my clients' experiences and my own, I have seen the fearlessness, raw strength, and unshakable sense of empowerment that these experiences leave in their wake—if we use various strategies to allow them to.

I love this amazing quote: "A woman is like a tea bag. If you want to find out how strong she is, put her in hot water." So, my fellow tea bag friend, while I don't know your particular challenge, something that shook you up, rocked your world, or created a sense of unease that just won't let up brought you here. Let's talk about that sense of unease first.

Have you heard the story about the frog and the boiling water? It is kind of gross, but here goes. If you drop a frog in to a pot of boiling water, the frog will immediately jump out because it will be acutely aware that it is in a dangerous situation and wants to be safe. If, however, you drop the frog in a pot of lukewarm water and then slowly turn up the heat, the frog will not be aware of the slow and subtle changes happening to it. The frog will not think to escape and will eventually boil and die without ever knowing how it happened.

This is what happens with a midlife crisis. Something is slowly changing within, and what used to work simply isn't anymore. What used to bring us joy is no longer bringing us joy. We have outgrown what used to entertain us, and who we have been just doesn't feel as though it is working for us anymore. Because change creates a shake-up, disrupting and dismantling all that has been familiar, we do all we can to ignore it through food, drugs, alcohol, work, TV, reckless behavior, or simply by keeping busy. These distractions temporarily numb us so we don't have to face what is at the root of our discontent. Unfortunately, the stakes get higher and higher over time as we become addicted to the behavior and need more of our drug of choice to get the same effect. Like a drug addict who needs more of the drug for the same high, we need more of our distraction to remain numb. That works for a while, but at some point, what we have been pushing aside gets too big to ignore. Should we decide to stop numbing ourselves and face it, a cascade of emotions and events usually begin. Personally, I believe these wake-up calls are wonderful opportunities and give us the chance to be, do, and create something spectacular before it is too late.

Do you want to see what you are distracting yourself from? Here are a few revealing questions to ask yourself. They are not meant to be easy or brushed over. Take your time with them, and most of all, be honest. You may find an unexpected revelation when you take these questions seriously, because they are designed to be very revealing. If you find that you would rather not answer them, that is an even bigger signal that there is something that needs your attention. Now, if you were sitting in my office, or if I were coaching you at a distance, I would have you answer the questions with me right now.

So let's get started, and I will be right here waiting. Let me know when you are done. ☺

A Few Revealing Questions to Ask Yourself

- What am I choosing to not face?
- What am I pretending to not see?
- What isn't working that I need to address?

- What uncomfortable thought keeps trying to get my attention?
- Am I being honest with myself about what I want and what is important to me?
- What am I sacrificing to keep the peace?
- What do I hope will just go away without me having to address it?
- Am I happy with the way things are? If not, am I willing to address something to change that?
- What will life look like in five years if I don't deal with this issue?
- What could life look like in five years if I deal with this starting now?

How did it go? What did you learn? Now you know what needs your attention, and it is nothing that food, TV, shopping, or any other type of distraction can cure. This is a great first step, and you have finally received the message your soul has been trying to tell you for a very long time.

If you have been hit by a life crisis such as an illness, tragedy, or trauma, I have another exercise for you. Please know that in your greatest struggles lie your greatest triumphs. I know this is hard to see now, but as one of my mentors says, "A seed of greatness is planted after every struggle."

The version of you now is very different from the version of yourself you are soon to become. You will be taking the best parts with you and leaving the outdated beliefs and behaviors behind, creating a new, empowered, and unshakable version of you in your future. I know it is hard to imagine now, but it will be clear soon. What would you like to feel? How would you like to live? What emotions would you like to feel every day? Who would you like to spend your time with? What would you like to see change in your life?

Please take the time right now to get a piece of paper or your journal. Once you have paper and pen in hand, write a letter to yourself (handwriting creates a different experience from typing, so please write by hand). The letter is to you, and it should lovingly and compassionately say that even though you are confused or in pain now, you are about to undergo a transformation that will create an updated version of yourself. You will do this by letting go of what hasn't been working or what you have outgrown and then replacing it with wisdom, strength, resilience, clarity, and confidence.

Remember, you are taking with you the parts of you that you love, that make you, you. You are just letting go of the old story, the pain, heartache, confusion, and self-doubt as your unshakable self begins to emerge.

PART 1: Willingness to Change And Grow

If we are determined to keep doing what we have been doing, we can only keep getting more of the same. It takes a new way of thinking, acting, and reacting to create a different result, and while we may not know what these ways are just yet, when we are willing, we can at least open the door to explore and be open to what these new ideas may be. In this space of willingness and readiness, you send out a message that you are ready to try something new, even if you are not the least bit sure of what that will be.

As you begin, please be willing to do things differently. What you have done up to now has gotten you here, and now it is time to heal and create your next chapter. With this willingness, you will see many amazing changes.

Everything I share with you in this book has been tested by me and my clients, and it creates results. Even the order in which you will be doing things is this way for a reason. You know the definition of insanity, right? It is doing the same thing over and over and expecting a different result. So I will be suggesting exercises and actions that are different from what you are doing now and possibly unfamiliar, but they are designed to help you to find clarity and heal.

Okay, here we go...

1: Help from Spirituality: How to Hear those Supernatural Secrets Whispering in Your Ear

We all have an internal guidance system, an internal GPS that guides, supports, and directs us at all times. It never gets tired, never decides it would rather be doing something else, and never stops working. Yet we often become so busy, stressed, and disconnected that we forget we are connected to something bigger than ourselves, and we can feel very alone. Whether we call this guidance system our soul, spirit, divine guidance, intuition, energy, God, Source, or whatever, this energy, this unseen intelligence, is a part of everything. It makes the flowers grow and it makes your heart beat. It makes birds know exactly when to fly south for the winter. If something is smart enough to do all that and so much more, isn't it safe to say that it has our backs and is smart enough to help us understand and find some meaning behind our life crises?

The problem is that we don't trust ourselves, so we disregard the messages we receive. We don't listen to the messages because they are not as loud as the voice of our inner critic (the ego) that relentlessly chats in our heads. We don't strengthen our intuition, our inner guide and connection to something bigger, so it doesn't have a strong internal presence we can easily sense and feel. But when you look back, you will find that there have been plenty of instances in your life when, if you trusted your gut, if you trusted that wise inner guide, it probably would have spared you some heartache. When you learn how to connect to that inner wisdom, how to strengthen it, and how to trust it, you can hear those supernatural secrets whispered in your ear. You will feel as though you have been spending time with a best friend you never knew you had, one who is always available, doesn't judge, doesn't criticize, and always has your best interest in mind.

Connecting with something bigger than us helps give us a sense of being grounded, especially when our foundation has been rocked. We feel as if we are not alone, that we are supported and guided as we make sense of our crisis or simply try to determine our next best steps. When we make this connection and begin to trust it, we understand how we are given these challenges to help us grow and to offer us a sense of perspective. Countless clients have become grateful for their messy divorces because now they are madly in love with their soul mates. Others are thankful they got fired from their jobs because it gave them the push they needed to start their own business doing the work they love. Still others are grateful for a diagnosis because it taught them to never take anything or anyone for granted as they now savor every moment of the day. (I am not saying this is the case with everyone, and I am by no means minimizing any trauma you have been through. Sometimes a crisis just hits, and it stinks—period. But even then, consider that even though you have been through something tragic, you deserve to heal and live a life of love and meaning.)

We can look at a crisis as a valuable lesson that an unseen, loving intelligence is trying to get us to learn. For example, have you ever noticed that you keep winding up with the same type of bad relationship or job? Believing in an intelligence that has your best interest in mind can change how you look at that. Imagine being in a relationship where your boundaries got crossed, you were disregarded and disrespected. After you had enough, you got out of the relationship, and although you are now with a different person, you find those same things happening again, and you feel the same way you did in your last relationship. You get out of that relationship and then attract someone new who is oddly similar to the last person. The very human side of you may think you are simply unlucky, can't find someone to love, and are destined to live a life going from one unhappy relationship to the next. When you connect to something bigger than yourself that you know has your best interest in mind, you can see this scenario in an entirely different way.

Here is what the same situation looks like from a different perspective. You have a few of those bad relationships, and the whole time, that loving intelligence is trying to let you know how worthy, deserving, lovable, and loved you are. You are just not getting the message, so the Universe keeps bringing you more and more "opportunities" to learn in the form of bad relationships. The relationships keep getting worse, and the poor treatment, the lack of love, the disrespect, and all that goes with a bad relationship keeps getting worse. You still don't get it, so the Universe calls in the big guns—the worst relationship you have had yet. You question yourself as you feel confused, hurt, and upset. Your self-esteem and confidence plummet, and these relationships are like bad dreams you can't escape from . . . until you finally get the frying-pan-to-the-head message of: "Oh! I get it! I deserve SO much better than this! I will *never* let myself be treated like this again. I am worthy, deserving, lovable, and loved." Bingo! Lesson learned, because you finally listened to the messages that your loving, wise guide has been trying to get you to see all along.

So how do you strengthen this bond? Get quiet and go within. Meditate, journal, pray, do a mindfulness practice, start a gratitude journal, do breathing exercises, or whatever daily practice you enjoy to start building that connection. It is all about bypassing the logical and analytical mind, because you can't access that connection through your conscious awareness, the logical, thinking part of your brain. It is through your feelings, not through your thinking, that you will receive these messages, so turn up the feeling and turn down the thinking. While there are many ways to access that connection, meditation is a powerful one.

Meditation offers countless benefits, including reducing stress and improving health. And just as there are many benefits to meditation, there are as many ways to meditate, so find what is right for you. It is the same with journaling. Journaling is an excellent way to see what is hiding deep within your subconscious mind, and you may discover feelings you never even knew you had as you start writing and letting go. For me personally, the combination of meditating and journaling is very powerful. I will do a meditation, trying as best as I can to quiet the chatter in my head, then ask myself a question and just start writing. Sometimes I am amazed at what shows up. This process has led to great insights, awareness, and healing.

There is no right or wrong here. All that matters is that you are willing to give it a try. Also, make a deal with yourself before you try anything else. It is so easy to say, "That won't work" or "I don't have time." That is your ego's way of keeping you stuck so that it stays in charge. Have a non-negotiable rule that you are not allowed to criticize a process until you have made it a habit and given it enough time to see first-hand if it works for you or not. Understand that just because something is odd or unfamiliar doesn't mean it doesn't work, it just means it is new and worth trying.

2: Forgiveness: Why It Is So Hard and How to Do It

There is simply no logic or reason behind why someone is treated unfairly or cruelly. We can't make sense of why someone contracts a disease, loses a loved one, gets fired from a job, or why they are lied to, cheated on, or betrayed. Why someone would consciously hurt another or commit a harmful act to others or themselves is beyond our understanding. This is where the healing power of forgiveness is needed more than ever.

Forgiveness is just a word until we need to do it. It is hard to do because it speaks a language the logical, rational mind doesn't understand. If you are a logical, rational person, you can go over something a million times and it will never, ever make sense to you why someone would physically, mentally, or emotionally hurt someone else. Why would they betray someone? Why would they abuse someone? Why would someone intentionally cause harm to someone in any way? It can never make sense to the logical mind, and because we can't make sense of it, we can't compartmentalize it. We don't know where to put it, so we can't put it away and put it behind us.

When it comes to forgiveness, we struggle with the anger, bitterness, resentment, and injustice of it all. We feel completely justified and filled with rage as we blame someone for their actions. When the idea of forgiveness comes up, we have thoughts such as: "If I forgive them, am I making it okay? Am I letting them off the hook? Am I sending out a message that it is okay to treat me that way? Am I setting myself up for it to happen again?" There is no justice, and we can't find the benefit of letting something so bad be okay, so we hold on to the pain of a transgression that occurred maybe decades ago, believing that our pain somehow shows that person how wrong or hurtful their actions were. Holding on to all of that pain takes your power from you and takes a huge toll on your body, your mind, and your life as it slowly chips away at your health, well-being, and sanity. You have probably heard that forgiveness isn't about the other person, it is all about you. This sounds nice, and you would like to believe it. Here is a radical concept to embrace for the sake of your health, growth, and healing: it's true.

You may have heard the saying that "refusing to forgive is like drinking poison and expecting the other person to die." Whoever hurt you, whatever that transgression was, I am sure it was painful, but that person may not be upset by it or may not even be aware of it. In fact, that person may not have had their life affected by it much at all. Your life, however, has been put completely on hold, and you have been paying the price for someone else's behavior for weeks, months, years, even decades after it happened. I am not minimizing your pain, and I have been there, so I know how much it hurts. But think about it. If your life is on hold because of someone else's actions, look at how much power that person still has over you. Who are you punishing at this point?

Let's say your parents did something horrific when you were a child. Now you are in your forties and because of your history with your parents, you do not have the relationships you want because you don't feel lovable. You do not have the life you want because you are consumed with thoughts of the past. You are not surrounding yourself with people who inspire you, because you don't feel worthy. You stay in a dead-end job because you feel that is all you deserve. Or let's say that someone treated you awfully in a relationship; they hurt you, and you just can't forgive them for their actions and behavior. As a result, you put up a wall and hang on to your pain for dear life. Yes, you are keeping out the bad guys, but you are keeping out the good guys, too.

When it comes to forgiveness, I always picture a trapeze. You are holding on to the bar with both hands, and the only way to move forward is by letting go with one hand and reaching for the new bar in front of you. Moving forward is what forgiveness gives you, but you can't go anywhere unless and until you let go. Holding on to that pain and those painful memories keeps *you* stuck and prevents you from going anywhere. When you let go, you are free to soar.

Walking around with all that anger, frustration, despair, bitterness, resentment, hopelessness, helplessness, and all the other emotions that go with a lack of forgiveness affects you not only mentally and emotionally, but physically, too. It suppresses your immune system, making you less resistant to illness and disease. It causes stress-related issues such as hormonal disturbances, digestive issues, accelerated aging, anxiety, muscle aches, joint pain, depression and more. So think about it. Not only has that person done whatever it is that they did, but as a result, you are walking around with all of these physical issues, too. Look at the amount of power that person still has over you because of how tightly you are holding onto the pain, allowing them and their actions to impact you in so many ways.

Now, I understand; you are completely justified in feeling the way you do, and if you told your story to anyone, I am sure they would agree. That is exactly why forgiveness is so hard. Everything in your logical, rational mind is screaming, "But that was so unfair, so wrong, so hurtful! See?!" Yes, you are right, and you can either have your story or your freedom. It will never make sense, and it will never be okay, but you have punished yourself enough. There is a saying; "Hurt people hurt people." The person who hurt you did what they did from the limited awareness, background, understanding, lack of self-love, and place they were in. It is not an excuse, but someone conscious, connected, evolved, and aware couldn't intentionally hurt a fly. It is time to forgive and heal.

Let's talk about self-forgiveness. Maybe you did something awful and you keep punishing yourself over and over again. From the limited space that you came from, from the limited awareness that you had at the time, you may have made some horrible decisions and hurt people in the process. This quote is for you: "If you knew better, you'd do better." Because of your actions, you may be feeling guilt, shame, and embarrassment, and you just can't move forward because of it. Now that you see the situation more clearly, you feel you don't deserve happiness. You don't deserve to feel better about yourself. You don't deserve to have a loving relationship because of what you did. What is *that* doing for you? That is not helping you or anybody else.

Think about it, though. If you forgive yourself, and because of that you do everything you can to make it right for whomever you hurt, aren't you now helping to make their life a little bit better? If you changed because of what you learned, aren't you now able to help other people because of it? Often, recognizing when we did something selfish or cruel or were on the receiving end of something horrible is when we transform, because we now see things so clearly. We get a wake-up call as we realize, "What was I thinking? What was I doing? What were my values, and what did I believe for me to behave that way?" That eye-opening moment of clarity can be the catalyst for the highest and best version of you to emerge, a version of you that is filled with integrity, compassion, and love. Punishing yourself doesn't help anyone. Forgive yourself, make it right, and make the world better because of what you have discovered.

Reading books on forgiveness; working with coaches, therapists, healers, and supportive friends and family; and practicing mantras, meditation, journaling, energy work and more can all be used to help you forgive. Try a few things out to find out what feels best for you to forgive and set yourself free.

3: Death and Rebirth: Shedding the Old, Embracing the New

We often have challenges that stem from a past hurt, whether from a divorce, betrayal, or struggle with a family member, friend, spouse, or business partner. We know it is in our best interest to find a way to move forward because there is certainly no benefit in replaying the event and the emotions that go with it hundreds (or thousands) of times in our heads. It is consuming, exhausting, bad for our health, and prevents us from seeing the beauty around us.

Maybe we are just tired of putting our needs on the back burner. We have given up so much for so long, and we just are not willing to do it anymore, but we don't know how to break the cycle. So we try a few things. We may yell, punch pillows, get support, or join a group and tell people about our hurt in the hope that it will ease the pain. We may choose a healthy outlet to help us, such as journaling, meditating, and exercising. We may choose unhealthy ways that keep us numb so we don't think about it—drinking, emotional eating, watching TV, diving into work—but the pain is still there, and it just won't go away.

Then we look for new strategies. We may try to let it go and make a conscious decision to cut those ties to the pain and the past hurt. We may try to forgive (as discussed in the last chapter) so we can take back our power, reclaim our resolve, and look at things with fresh eyes. While these options can help, I found something else that worked for me, and I want to share it with you.

Sometimes the pain just pierces through us, and while our highest selves may know these choices are all great options, we are simply too stuck in our smaller selves to embrace them fully. We are so consumed with our story and drowning in our waves of pain that we can't imagine ever feeling better. When these choices aren't working for you, here is a concept to consider: *death and rebirth*.

Before I explain what I mean, I will describe something I have seen many times. Once we have our stories of illness, heartbreak, abuse, and so on, they become a part of us, almost like a second skin. Our stories are familiar because we have repeated them to ourselves and others so many times that they have become who we are. While getting rid of our painful stories so we feel better seems like a no-brainer, we often hold on to them with a vice grip. Why? Fear. If this is who we have become (the diabetic, the one who always gets the short end of the stick, the unluckiest person alive, the "big" one, and so on) and then we get rid of it, who will we be? How will we be viewed, categorized, and seen? If we don't know who we would be without this identity, we will hold on to it.

I know this sounds crazy, but I have worked with many women who held on to a disease because they became so familiar with life with that disease. Some clients held on to excess weight because they knew how their lives "worked" with the excess weight on. I have worked with people who have held on to abusive relationships because their victim story could remain solidly in place. I have had clients who played out their martyr story for so long that it felt completely normal to allow others to take advantage of them. I am not suggesting that any of these were conscious decisions, but if we don't figure out who we would be without the issue, we may subconsciously hang on to it until we do.

Let's say you are tired of your story and all the side effects. You are ready to put it to rest. How can the idea of death and rebirth work for you?

Sometimes you need full closure to move forward, put the issue behind you, and move on. To me, that means the death of the old you, the old relationship, and the old ways that created something you now don't like. It means the death of what you had been accepting but are no longer willing to accept. It means the death of who you were at the time, knowing you did the best you could with the information you had access to.

Bringing that old part of you, the relationship, the situation, and the pain to a full stop allows for the birth of something totally new. Maybe it means the rebirth of a stronger, wiser, and more confident you. Maybe it is the birth of a new relationship (either with the person you are struggling with or with someone new) based on respect, support, and trust. Maybe it is the birth of a new way to communicate, a new perspective, a new understanding, a new way to go about your day.

Nature is perfect. In the fall season, things close down and come to an end, and in the spring season, everything has a brand new opportunity to start again with renewed beauty, strength, and magnificence. So do you.

If you are trying to let go and forgive and still feel stuck, the concept of death and rebirth may just be worth a try. This means envisioning putting an unhappy situation to rest; you can even do it in a big ceremonial way to make it more official. It may mean a full-blown "dark night of the soul" experience in which things get so dark, so painful, so consuming, and so overwhelming that you can't imagine sinking any further. It is the moment of truth, the moment you give up, give in, continue to numb yourself, stuff your pain—or the moment that your body, mind, and soul exquisitely align and come together with the sole intention of helping you climb.

Until that moment, it is like this. Picture your head (ego) saying one thing and tugging on one arm while your heart (soul) is saying something else and pulling on the other arm. Your body is caught right in the middle and is paying the price with failing health, fatigue, and overwhelm as you go back and forth with growing feelings of frustration, confusion, and pain.

Your dark-night-of-the-soul experience may happen when, after all that tugging and pulling, after all that chaos in your head, you can't take it anymore and finally decide something has to change. It is time to make a decision. You can't put yourself through this for one minute more. You make a decision at that instant to let your soul win, and from that moment on, you put yourself on a new path and change the direction of your life. This is the breakdown before the breakthrough, and the breakthrough marks the rebirth of the new you and the death of the old you. You are now ready to transform and

become unshakable.

Part 2: Mindset

If you are already conditioned to feel hopeless, helpless, depressed, filled with a sense of scarcity, and lack experience when you enter a life crisis or a midlife crisis, what tools do you have to support you to help you get though it and make sense out of your situation? Your crisis will throw you for a loop for sure, and you will need all the mental and emotional strength you can muster to find ways over, through, and around your new challenge. Even if you haven't gone through a crisis, a healthy way to think is always beneficial. Having a mindset that is programmed with a sense of "Okay, this sucks, but we'll figure it out and get through it" has an element of strength, resilience, and grit that will surely help you in taking the steps you need to in order to get you through your challenge.

Since your thoughts create your actions, your actions create your behaviors, your behaviors create your habits, and your habits create your life, it is time to get rid of that stinkin' thinkin' for a new way to think that will take you where you want to go. Ready? Here we go...

4: Change Your Thoughts, Change Your Life

Have you ever noticed that you wanted to make changes in a certain area, then made those changes but the results were short-lived? It's not your fault. We often think that if we change our behavior, we will have a different result. That is a great start in the right direction, but there is more to it. Those results are short-lived because unless we change the belief that created the behavior in the first place, we will eventually go back to what is comfortable and familiar . . . even if it stinks. We also do what I call "rear view mirror thinking." That is when you keep looking in the small rear view mirror of your past instead of looking at the huge front windshield of your future that is right in front of you. Imagine driving like that, just staring at the rear view mirror as you drove instead of looking in front of you. You wouldn't get very far. Instead of looking at where you can go and the possibility ahead, you may be busy viewing, ruminating, and recreating where you have been. You wouldn't drive like that, but we sure live that way sometimes. Your belief system drives every thought, behavior, action, and habit you have, so if you want any change to last, then you need to change from rear view mirror thinking to front windshield thinking, as well as change your beliefs at the root.

So what is a belief? A belief is simply the repetition of an idea from someone you trust. That's it. This means that someone you trusted said something (or you said it to yourself) enough times that it became your belief. It doesn't make it good or bad, right or wrong, and it doesn't necessarily make the belief true, but it does make it yours. A belief is not necessarily a fact, either. A fact is something that doesn't change. Let's take gravity, for example. If you throw something up, it is going to come down. Gravity is a fact. A belief, on the other hand, can be thoughts such as, "I am so stupid." "I will never be in a loving relationship." "I will never be debt-free." These beliefs can be dismantled with a new way of thinking. We may think beliefs are facts, but as long as there is a possibility of them not being true, then they are only beliefs and can be challenged and changed.

How do these beliefs get started in the first place? When something makes an impression on us, we lay down a "track" for it in our brains. Over time, as we repeat the thought and infuse it with feeling, that track gets strengthened and solidified. As this happens, we start believing in that thought more and more. Through repetition, the brain begins to think, "Oh, you want me to keep repeating this? Okay, here is what we will do. I will just slip this idea into your subconscious mind so that the belief is an automatic program that repeats and runs all the time. Then you can go ahead and do all the other things you need to do." This track may have been laid down by a traumatic event or something that just made an impression on you. For example, maybe when you were little, you had some breaking news to tell your mom. You ran into the kitchen, but your mom was on the phone, so she gave you one of those "shh" motions with her hand. She shushed you. She was just trying to hear the other person on the phone, but that was the moment when you laid down an "I'm not worthy" track. Or maybe you were in a school play, and when you looked out into the audience, you didn't see your dad. You didn't know it, but the traffic made it impossible for him to be there in time. But because you didn't see him in the audience, at that moment you laid down an "I'm not important" track. See how this can happen?

Now, if you have repeated these ideas so often that they have become well-worn tracks in your brain, and you believe you are not worthy or important, you will find confirming evidence that supports your beliefs so you can say, "See? I told you so!" because your mind always wants to prove you right. Here is where we get into trouble. We don't question our beliefs. We think, "This is who I am, and it's true." No it's not; it is a belief. Your beliefs have been driving your choices, actions, and behaviors, but they can be changed.

It gets worse. We have between sixty thousand and eighty thousand thoughts a day. Let's say you laid down an "I'm not worthy" track or an "I'm not important" track. Now imagine repeating some form of those beliefs, say—let's take a low number—around five thousand times a day. Think about it. If you did anything five thousand times a day, what would happen?

If you repeat some form of "I'm not worthy" or "I'm not important" five thousand times a day and you are always hunting for confirming evidence to support that belief over and over again, can you see how drastically that would impact your life? It is time to look at what you have been telling yourself. Do your beliefs serve you? If they do, great. But if they are keeping you safe, stuck, and small, it is time to let them go and set them free.

Your beliefs affect everything. If you believe you are not worthy, you may not be as particular about whom you allow and don't allow into your life. You may settle for any job that comes along instead of doing work that feels rewarding and fulfilling. See how it shows up? If you are not sure what you believe, take a look around you. Your life is a complete representation of the beliefs you hold. Your beliefs got you to where you are now, so to create something different, you are going to need a different set of beliefs.

How do you do that? One way is to build bridges…

5: Building Beliefs by Building Bridges

Affirmations are great. Many people find them helpful to change the way they think, but many of my clients have struggled with affirmations because some of them seemed so far-fetched and unrealistic that they felt as though they weren't being honest with themselves when they said them. Or they felt as though what they were saying was so far from where they currently were that it was hard to imagine the affirmation ever becoming their reality. With that, I came up with the idea of building bridges instead. What is a bridge? A bridge is a believable statement that we can grab on to in order to start laying down a new, empowering, and believable belief. Once that new, empowering belief is laid down, we create another bridge, bringing us steadily closer to what we want.

For example, consider an obese woman who weighs four hundred pounds. Over a period of years, possibly decades, she has said some version of "I'm so fat" countless times. Because she has said it so many times, she has an "I'm so fat" track laid down in her brain that is continuously running without her conscious awareness. If she were to look in the mirror and say, "I am a lean, mean, 125-

pound woman," her mind would respond with, "No, you're not" and kick the thought right out.

Because she has been so conditioned to think "I'm so fat," she may not even realize she is thinking it. She thinks it all day long: when she gets dressed, when she looks in the mirror, when she passes a window and sees her reflection. She thinks and subconsciously says some version of "I'm so fat" all day long.

Now let's say she starts eating healthier every day. She eats cleaner, has fewer processed foods, drinks more water, and steadily moves toward her goal. She is still overweight and probably thinks she is still far from her goal, but it is fair and believable for her to say, "I'm eating healthier every day." That is a bridge; a believable and empowering statement because it is true. If she starts to catch herself thinking "I'm so fat" and remembers to say the bridge of "I'm eating healthier every day," through repetition and consistency, she will start to lay down a new track in her brain.

Initially, this process can be awkward and uncomfortable. She is probably not going to remember to say the bridge at first, and she may not realize at all how often she thinks the disempowering belief of "I'm so fat." Eventually, however, if she stays with it, the new, empowering belief of "I'm eating healthier every day" becomes more comfortable and even automatic. The old track of "I'm so fat" loses its charge, the new track eventually takes hold and takes over, and that is how you literally change your mind.

How do you create your own bridges? Nothing happens without awareness, so the first step is to become aware of the subconscious programming that drives just about everything you say and do. The easiest way I know to do this is to write down these phrases:

I am so . . . I can't . . . I will never . . .

Now, without judging, critiquing, or monitoring yourself, free-flow your responses and see what shows up. Just keep writing, and you will find major blocks that have been in the way of creating the body, relationships, mindset, and life you want. For example, you may write: "I am so lazy." "I can't get organized." "I will never get rid of this pain." Since your brain always wants to prove you right, you will see why those tracks you have laid down have led to certain outcomes. Also, as you write, don't be surprised if you hear the voice of the person who originally said these things to you or the voice of that nagging inner critic.

Once you are done, start creating bridges, especially for the ones that hold the most negative emotion and charge for you. Remember, a bridge has to be believable enough for you to grab onto until it is a new, empowering belief. Going from "I'm so lazy" to "I am the most motivated person on the planet" may not work, so what would be more empowering? Maybe "I am motivated to do the things that interest me" would work. I find that it is often best just to crack open the door to the old belief by questioning it, which may look something like this: "What if I am not so lazy?" Imagine if, every time you called yourself lazy, you said your bridge of "What if I am not so lazy" instead? Over time, that questioning would lay down a new track, and you would actually start questioning that maybe you are not so lazy after all. Once that track is successfully laid down and you truly believe you may not be lazy, *then* you can become the most motivated person on the planet. ☺

Just a few weeks ago, I realized I had a disempowering belief myself, and it was impacting many areas of my life. I had a belief that I had been saying to myself, my kids, and others my entire life: "Nothing good comes easy." I had never before put it together, but whenever there was a problem with an appliance in my house, I was that person who heard, "I'm sorry, Ms. Silber, but we've never seen that before." When there was a problem with an unresolved computer issue, I would hear, "That is the oddest thing. I'll call my senior manager, because I have never seen anything like that." When there was a problem with a simple solution that just about anyone was able to see but me, I would hear, "Debi, what the heck! Why is this so hard for you to understand?" Yep, that was me. One day, it struck me like a two-by-four to the head: I realized I set things up to be difficult because I believed nothing good comes easy! My mind always wants to prove me right, and I had a truckload of confirmation to prove it.

I did an experiment and created a bridge of "What if good things *can* come easy?" I even kept a little journal called *Good Things Coming Easy*, with Day 1, Day 2, and so on. Within days I started finding things the old version of myself would never have found because, well, that would have been too easy. I had a problem on my computer that could have erased a huge amount of work, but I did something and fixed it. I spoke with an event planner about a detail regarding an upcoming event I was speaking at, and it was absolutely no problem to change it. Good things were coming easy!

What are your disempowering beliefs? Take a look at how they have held you back. Then create bridges and start creating the results you want.

Before you start thinking that this is too hard and you can't do it, know that you have done this many times before, and I can prove it. Remember when you used to believe in the tooth fairy? (My apology if I just ruined it for you). That was you believing something. When the belief no longer served you, you set it free. Now is the time to do the same thing. Find out what your beliefs are, and if they don't move you closer to what you want, then just as you did with the tooth fairy, set that belief free and replace it with one that will serve you so much better.

6: A Step-by-Step Process to Reveal the Ultimate Version of You

In this process of becoming unshakable, we have been working on creating the strongest and best version of you. But what does the ultimate version of you look like? What qualities do you have? How do you spend your time? Who do you spend your time with? When you find this out, it becomes your bullseye, your target, your direct point of what to shoot for and work toward. It is like planning a trip. Let's say you want to go on a fabulous trip, but you didn't get a ticket in advance. You go to the airport and say to the ticket agent, "I want to go on an incredible trip." Well, that's nice, and the agent would probably say, "Um, okay, where to?" If you respond with, "I don't know; I just want to go somewhere really good," it isn't likely that you would get very far. If, however, you said, "I want to go to Maui," then you can get your ticket to Maui because you have a target. You are on your way to a beautiful place. That is what this visioning activity can do for you.

You might say, "This is silly. I'm not going to bother with it. I'll just skip this chapter and read the next one." But I will tell you, after having done this activity many times with groups, from stages, and with private clients who have taken it seriously, I have seen it change lives. It can really be that transformative, so I hope you will join me and play full-out.

Don't overthink, don't judge, and don't critique yourself. Just get a piece of paper and pen ready, put your piece of paper and pen aside for later, and take a nice, deep breath. I will ask you a series of questions to create pictures in your mind. I want you to visualize the version of you that matches the questions I ask. Okay, now get comfortable, take a deep breath, and start picturing the ultimate you as I ask these questions...

The Visioning Activity

Visualize yourself at your physical, mental, and emotional best, your personal and professional best, and start settling into that space. Once you have settled into that vision, picture your health. What is your health like at your physical, mental, and emotional best, your personal and professional best?

Once you have visualized your health, picture your energy. What is your energy like at your physical, mental, and emotional best, your personal and professional best?

Once you have pictured your health and your level of energy, visualize your body. What does your body look like at your physical, mental, and emotional best, your personal and professional best? See what your body looks like with that level of health and energy, when you are at your physical, mental, and emotional best, your personal and professional best.

Once you have visualized what your body looks like with that level of health and energy, imagine what you are wearing. What are you wearing when you are at your physical, mental, and emotional best, your personal and professional best? Is there a certain style, a certain designer? Specific colors? See what you are wearing when you are at your physical, mental, and emotional best, your personal and professional best. What are you wearing with that body at that level of health and energy, at your physical, mental, and emotional best, your personal and professional best?

Once you have pictured what you are wearing on that body with that level of health and energy, visualize what you are doing when you are at your physical, mental, and emotional best, your personal and professional best. What are you doing as you wear that outfit on that body with that level of health and energy?

Once you have visualized what you are doing with that outfit on that body with that level of health and energy, imagine who is with you. Is there one person or are many people with you? Who is with you when you are at your physical, mental, and emotional best, your personal and professional best? Who is with you as you are doing what you are doing, wearing what you are wearing on that body with that level of health and energy? You are at your physical, mental, and emotional best, your personal and professional best.

Once you imagine who is with you, whether many people, one person, or no one, imagine that you are wrapping up whatever it is you are doing and that person or those people are leaving. What are they saying about having spent time with you in this way? What are the words they say and the feelings they have after spending time with you in this way, when you were doing what you were doing, wearing that outfit on that body with that level of health and energy? You are at your physical, mental, and emotional best, your personal and professional best.

Once you have visualized all of that, imagine that you have wrapped up what you have been doing and you are getting ready to go. How do you feel having spent time in that way with that person or those people while you were doing what it was you were doing, wearing that outfit on that body with that level of health and energy? How do you feel about contributing in that way?

Once you have pictured the boldest, brightest, clearest vision you can, once you can clearly see what you were doing and who you were with, what you were wearing, the body you had, and the health and energy you had, once that vision is bold and bright, vibrant and clear, slowly open your eyes and write down exactly what you saw.

What did you see? How did you look? What were you doing? How did you feel?

What you saw, maybe for the very first time, was the real you— *that* is who you are. That is you without the limiting beliefs. That is you without the habits that don't serve you. That is you with you out of the way. Aren't you awesome?

You never would have seen that version of you if it didn't exist. What you saw is your bullseye and the clear target of the *ultimate* and *unshakable* you. Do you want proof? Look around at the space you are in now. *Every single thing that exists* went through three steps. First it was envisioned, then it was expressed, and then it was created.

It works the same way with you. You envisioned what you want, you wrote it down and expressed it, and now it is just a matter of creating it. Now that you have done steps one and two, how do you get to step three? Let's track back to see what you have to do to get there so you can take strategic action toward it.

Let's say you envisioned a strong, empowered woman with a lean, fit, healthy body. For you to have that body, you had to start working out and eating healthier. Get the idea? I have done this with women who picture themselves with a new hairstyle or different hair color. In order for them to have that cut and color, they had to go to their hairdresser and get it done.

One of my clients imagined herself on a stage and wearing a beautiful black-and-white outfit. Her next step was to go out and find that outfit. Step by step, this is how you become. You have heard the saying, "Fake it 'til you make it," but this is different. We are not talking about faking it here, we are talking about seeing it and then taking daily actions to become it. Of course, do what you can. I remember working with a client who pictured herself mountain biking. While her body wasn't in the physical condition it needed to be in order to mountain bike, she found what she could do immediately and joined an online mountain biking group. What can you do to make your vision real and bring yourself toward what you imagined?

I was working with a client in California, and we were also friends on Facebook. We did this visioning activity, and she clearly described an image of her new self. About three months later, she posted a picture on Facebook with the caption, "What do you think about my new look?" I got chills. I got chills because she looked *exactly* like what she had described to me a few months earlier. I wasn't going to call her out on Facebook, so I texted her. "Do you remember that vision you described to me a few months ago?" About ten minutes later she texted back, "OMG!!!!!" She had become that vision.

This activity helps you become empowered, too, because that ultimate version of you has every answer you need. She knows how to eat, work out, think, act, behave, and react in a healthy way, so why not consult with her? Imagine that something comes up and instead of having a typical reflexive response, you think, "Hmm, what would Ultimate (insert your name) do?" How would she handle a situation or work through a problem?

I know you may not believe this yet, but you have all those answers, and if you start from this moment forward acting, behaving, and responding as that highest and best version of you, watch how fast you will become her. I consistently see this happen with my clients. They are blown away with how they show up when they respond from that place, whether they are getting over a relationship, trying to create a new one, changing careers, working on health issues, dealing with an annoying relative, or handling any number of situations. Responding and making decisions as the highest and ultimate version of you is a game changer.

7: Strengthening the Gatekeeper

Even though you are creating the highest and best version of you, toxic thoughts and that nagging, negative self-talk may still try to sabotage your efforts. Have you ever noticed that you can take steps and start to make progress, then slip and fall back? Sometimes those negative thoughts you were trying to manage come back stronger than ever, and you feel you are getting worse instead of better. If you can relate, you may need to strengthen your gatekeeper. Here is what I mean.

Imagine a gatekeeper of your mind: a strong, powerful force standing guard and deciding which thoughts are allowed to enter and which ones need to go. Of course, the gatekeeper wants to let in the positive thoughts and keep out the negative (kind of like a big bodyguard powerfully protecting someone). Now imagine that the gatekeeper is constantly being bombarded with so many negative thoughts that the gatekeeper begins to weaken. Sure, the gatekeeper is still trying to do its job, but it is slowly getting beaten down by the constant and unrelenting negativity that just keeps coming in.

Eventually, the gatekeeper gets weak and can no longer find the strength to manage all of those negative thoughts, which have now set up camp, (like a bunch of wild five-year-olds in a classroom without the teacher), in the cozy new home of your mind. Sure, the positive thoughts come in, but they don't stand a chance, as these negative thoughts have now become an army of negative forces that have taken out the gatekeeper and slowly polluted your mind.

So what do you do? Of course, the first step is awareness. We can't change anything if we are not aware of it. If this is what has been happening with you, consider this idea: what we feed, grows. When we feed those negative thoughts, we actually help them get stronger, and chances are they have been getting plenty of food for thought. These thoughts have been slowly polluting and poisoning your mind, and since thoughts lead to feelings that lead to behaviors that lead to habits that lead to your life—well, just look where feeding those thoughts is taking you. It is time to stop this madness, strengthen the gatekeeper, and slowly detox your mind from this pollution.

It starts with compassion for your gatekeeper, who has been beaten down by those negative thoughts taking over. Start to heal your gatekeeper by refusing to feed the thoughts. Stay with it, and over time, your gatekeeper will regain its strength and be able to stand guard and protect you once again.

Where do these thoughts come from? They often come from the relationships we have with the people in our lives. Stay with me, because we are taking on that topic next.

Part 3: Relationships

There is a saying, "People are in your life for a reason, a season, or a lifetime." Who you spend your time with can impact just about every aspect of your life, from the thoughts you think to the things you do and the habits you have. When it comes to healing from a life crisis or navigating a midlife crisis effectively, those relationships become even more revealing than ever and can show us the people to move toward, the people to steer clear of, and the people we want to surround ourselves with when we need support and want to become our best. During these times, we also benefit from those who have blazed the path we are ready to walk on and those who can offer guidance, direction, and support as we determine our next steps. Are you unsure of who is helping or harming your efforts to become unshakable? It will become clear in the next section.

8: How to Climb Out of the Crab Bucket

Consider the people in your life. Who do you spend your time with and how do they make you feel? Do you spend time with people who are inspiring, energizing, positive, and optimistic? Or do you spend time with energy vampires who drain the life out of you? Motivation speaker Jim Rohn said that we are the average of the five people we spend the most time with. Studies show that when we spend enough time with certain people, we will have similar salaries, similar lifestyle habits, and more. This is a good thing when the people around us have habits and behaviors we want to emulate ourselves, but it is not a good thing when we take on the actions and behaviors of others whose beliefs and behaviors hold us back from being, doing, and having what we want.

Surrounding yourself with people who drain and deplete you reminds me of a bucket of crabs. Have you ever seen a bucket of crabs? All these crabs are swarming around the bottom of the bucket, and you don't even need to put a lid on the bucket to keep them in. They don't realize that they can get out, and their fellow crab friends don't see it, either. For them, it seems as though life exists only within that bucket. But every once in a while, there is that hopeful crab, that one crab with a dream, that tries to climb up the side. It believes in a chance at a better life outside the bucket, so it makes the decision to try to climb up the side and be free. What happens next? There is always some crab down in the bucket, angry, resentful, and bitter that it is stuck there. It sees the crab start to climb and immediately snatches onto its claw, bitterly thinking, "Nope! If I'm not going, then you're not going, either!" Then it pulls the crab right back down into the crab bucket with the rest of the crabs.

So look at the people you spend your time with and ask yourself this question. Are you hanging out in the crab bucket? If you are, are those the people who will help you create the life and lifestyle that you want? I can tell you personally and from the thousands of women I have worked with that you will not find the happiness you are looking for if you are hanging out in that crab bucket. Be that hopeful crab—keep climbing, and get out of there.

Think about it. If you are trying to create something magnificent and everyone around you is negative, critical, judgmental, and pessimistic, then believing in your own new path and plan is going to be twice as hard. The naysayers (who may mean well) will have you doubting why you ever thought your idea was viable in the first place. If these are the only people in your life, then without a rock-solid resolve, your self-doubt can't help but rear its head.

Here's an example. A few years ago, I was preparing to put on a live event. I met up with a wonderful group of stay-at-home moms. Now, I am not touching that working mom versus stay-at-home mom debate with a ten-foot pole. I am a total believer that every mom knows what is best for her family and for herself. I also know that raising my four kids often made me a little cuckoo, and having my business sometimes helped me stay sane. Anyway, the "What's new with you?" question came up, and I started talking about my upcoming event, explaining that it was a chance for women to take a day off of work, do some personal development, and network with others. I was excited to share my vision and dream. I must have been rambling, and then I started having that sinking feeling, as I slowly realized I may have just shared the weirdest plan they had ever heard. Within minutes, I heard things like, "Who is going to take time off of work to go to a personal development event?" "Ninety-seven dollars?! That's a lot of money for a ticket!" and "A whole day? That's a long time for someone to sit there and learn." As I sat there taking in their well-meaning advice meant to spare me expense, embarrassment, and disappointment, I started to think, *I still have time to cancel the event. I still have time to cut my losses, and I have time to change my plans.* I thought, *What have I been thinking? I can't sell tickets to this event. Who is going to go? Who is really going to take the time to go to something like this? This is crazy! What was I thinking?*

When I left, I raced back to my office. I was in a mastermind group, and we had a private Facebook page to brainstorm, offer support, and suggest ideas. I typed furiously. "I just left a group, and I talked about my event, and I'm thinking of canceling it." Then I started listing all the reasons why I should cancel. Within minutes, I was flooded with responses such as, "A one-day event? It should be two days!" "Ninety-seven dollars? Holy smokes! It's worth way more than that!" "It's in New York? I wish I lived closer! I'd be there in a second!"

You see? If I surrounded myself only with group A, I probably would have canceled my event, but because I also surrounded myself with group B, I did the event, and it was wonderful. It led to great opportunities, and many important lessons were learned.

Who are you surrounding yourself with? Are they keeping you safe, stuck, and small? Are they having you question yourself and your ability to forge a new path? Your relationships with these people may have worked when you thought and believed a certain way, but now that you see things differently, things need to change.

Let's say you are in a relationship and it "worked" because you had a low self-esteem and a poor self-image. Because of that, your partner has felt safe and secure. Now you start changing your habits, which leads you to lose weight, become fit, and have more confidence. As a result, your partner becomes threatened, jealous, and insecure. I have worked with so many women who say to me, "Debi, I don't get it. I lose the weight and then sabotage myself once I start looking and feeling good. What's up with that?" Of course, it can be a food issue, but as I start asking questions such as, "What happens in your relationship when you start feeling more confident?" I will then get the familiar deer-in-the-headlights look as they start to realize that this is the point where their partner feels threatened. Instead of rocking the boat, they will put the weight back on so the relationship can continue to "work." But does it?

As you change, your spouse, partner, or food buddy friend, sees your changes and is then faced with a few issues themselves. First, they may feel as if they are at risk of losing you now that you are off in this new and healthy direction. Second, your changes subtly force them to look at their own habits, which they may not want to look at or be ready to face. So, what we often do is sabotage ourselves, we shrink, and stay small so we don't make the other person uncomfortable. Are you doing that?

I have seen this play out in business, too. Many brilliant women have ideas that could make a huge impact in the work they do, within the organizations they work for, and with the people who would benefit as a result. Instead of being bold, taking a chance, and sharing their vision, which could dramatically improve their current result or change the direction of their work for the better, they shrink so that no one feels threatened and uncomfortable. We can do this for a while, but when we keep sacrificing ourselves so that others feel comfortable, we often become resentful and slowly give up on our visions. We begin to doubt ourselves too, which only increases the resentment. Here is something important to note. It's not the other person's fault. Sacrificing your growth to keep them comfortable was a choice you made and it may have worked well for a period of time. But, if you are meant and ready to grow, halting your progress for the sake of someone else's comfort is a short-term solution that leads to long-term pain.

Now, I get it if you are in a place in life where certain things just aren't possible, but here is where you choose your regrets. For example, many times over the years I have wanted to do things in my business, but it would have meant too much time away from my family. I am not going to lie; it was often incredibly frustrating to be so passionate about something and yet intentionally keep the idea on hold. There were years when I felt like I had one foot on the gas pedal and the other on the brake, because if I let up on the brake, I would spend way too much time working and miss time with my kids that I wouldn't be able to get back. I would question myself as I said no to opportunities that could have been great for business but bad for my family. Did I always make the right choices? No, but checking in with a regret I could live with was something that worked for me.

What regrets will you choose? Perhaps you have been sacrificing your health and happiness for someone else's need to feel in control or secure. When you see it clearly and become unwilling to live that way anymore, that is often the catalyst behind the self-induced life crisis or midlife crisis we have been talking about. This is why we did the visioning activity in the last section. The woman you envisioned knows what is best because she is the best and highest version of you.

It is time to check in with the ultimate and unshakable version of you. If you didn't do the visualizing activity, please go back and do it now, because checking in will help you see exactly what and who you need in your life. Do the people around you help you grow? Do they support you becoming your best? If not, are you willing to keep things as is in order to keep the peace? Or are your heart and soul crying out for more? Change is scary, and that is exactly why we distract and numb ourselves—so that we can avoid these big changes . . . until we can't.

Becoming aware of what you have been sacrificing in order to keep things as they have been is truly a shift, as you are now faced with many options and decisions you weren't even aware you had. You see things differently, and you are at a new level of awareness that you can't undo. This growth can definitely shake up others as it simultaneously rocks you to your core. But in that shake-up lies your greatest growth. Be patient with yourself. Outgrowing anything can be uncomfortable. Picture a growing child who is forced to wear the same clothes every day that simply don't fit anymore. It may work for a while, but at some point, things just need to change.

Changes can range from simple to extreme, and no one knows what you need more than you do. Maybe in addition to those already in your life, you simply need some new, growth-oriented people in your life who help you expand and adding these new relationships can satisfy that need. Maybe you need to set new boundaries with a partner who can better support you on your new path with an updated set of rules in place. Perhaps you have outgrown your current relationships, and just like those small clothes on that growing child, you just can't make them fit anymore.

Take your time with making these choices, and get support if you need it. Everyone, and I mean everyone, who comes into your life is there intentionally. They are in your life to teach you something vital for your own growth and evolution. They are there to show you what you are made of, what you are willing to tolerate, and to show you parts of yourself that need healing. They are in your life to help you grow your wings so that you can become the healthiest and most fabulous version of yourself...especially the people who have hurt you the most. I swear, it has been the people who have hurt me the most who have been my greatest teachers. They have taught me invaluable lessons about life, resilience, support, and love, even if the lesson I learned was what *not* to do. They have given me great pain and enormous and unshakable strength. Remember, everyone is in your life for a reason, a season, or a lifetime. What roles do your relationships serve? Take a close look as you give thanks for the ones who are steadfastly by your side as well as the ones who have taught you your most painful yet most valuable life lessons.

9: Romantic Relationships: What Do You Need Now?

Let's talk about love, partnerships, and marriage. Now, I am not going to say that my marriage has been perfect by any means; in fact, I will be writing a book on huge life lessons, including that exact topic, down the road. What I will share here is that in my own experience of being with my husband for thirty-two years (married for twenty-five) as well as working with countless women in and out of relationships, I have learned some important lessons worth sharing.

One lesson I learned is why I can't stand the statement, "You complete me." That, my friend, is a setup for disaster. I know it sounds romantic, but here is the problem. If you don't complete yourself first, if you always look for outside confirmation to show you your worth, and if you need others to confirm that you are deserving of love, what happens if they stop confirming? If your day is okay only when someone says the right thing, wakes up on the right side of the bed, or sees and acknowledges how great you are, what happens when they fail to do those things? I am not saying that those thoughtful, loving actions should stop, and in fact, I believe there shouldn't be a day that goes by when you are not recognized and appreciated for how great you are. What I am saying is that it is no one else's job to make you feel worthy, loved, beautiful, or lovable. That is your job, and when you do all you can to feel those things, you become complete.

Think about it. Say you feel that you are lacking in some way and you want someone to love you so you can believe that you are lovable. You meet someone who fills that need, but your belief that you are lovable is completely contingent on that person's perspective. Why are we willing to give our power away like that with something as important as feeling worthy of being loved? You see, placing your belief in how lovable you are in someone else's hands creates a flimsy and unstable foundation, because knowing that you are lovable is then out of your control, putting you in a completely reactive position. It is like instead of being the driver, you have made yourself a passenger, hoping that whoever happens to take the wheel knows how to drive.

I am not saying that it is not wonderful to have someone take great care of you and meet lots of your needs. In fact, that is a beautiful part of a relationship when it is built on solid ground. But here I am talking about giving someone else the responsibility to make you feel whole; that's your job.

Let's look at another scenario. Say that you do the work to become your physical, mental, emotional, psychological, and spiritual best (which this book is hoping to help you accomplish). As a result, you feel confident, empowered, vibrant, healthy, worthy, lovable, and secure. With those qualities firmly in place, now you meet someone. Since like energy attracts like energy, it is likely that that person feels those same things too, and brings that and more to the table. So instead of two halves coming together to create one whole (as in the "you complete me" statement), two wholes create a powerhouse couple! See the difference?

We enter into and stay in relationships for many reasons, from falling in love and finding our soul mates to not wanting to be alone, settling for the best we think we can get, having someone help with the bills, not wanting to disappoint anyone, not being the only one in your group still without a partner and everything else in between. If you are in a relationship, look at the legs it is standing on. Are they firm, strong, and solid? If you are not in a relationship and want to be in one, please take the time to work on you first. I have seen too many times how starting a relationship when you are in a low place and then doing the work to change how you look, feel, and live isn't fair to either of you. The person you meet from that place of low energy may only be compatible while you are in that low-energy place. The person you are becoming may not be the least bit attracted to that person you met when you were not feeling your best. So for the sake of you both, do the work now to become your best, then watch an entirely different caliber of person enter your world.

One final note before we leave this section on relationships and support. Our relationships aren't just good or bad for us mentally and emotionally. They impact our health, too. Loving, nurturing, supportive people actually boost and support the immune system. On the other hand, people who are negative, critical, judgmental, and pessimistic suppress the immune system, making us less resistant to illness and disease. As long as you are looking closely at your relationships to see how they may be helping or harming you, look at how they may be impacting your health, too . . . which is exactly what we are taking on next, in Part 4.

PART 4: HEALTH

When you are reeling from your life crisis, creating a lean, fit, and healthy body may be the last thing on your mind. But when you are faced with a challenge, having a healthy body can help make your next steps much easier. From having more energy to bounce back from an illness to having more confidence when your self-esteem has been rocked by a betrayal, having your health will serve as a benefit on your journey to becoming unshakable. In this section, I will show you how all the stress you have been feeling from your life challenge may have created a less-than-desirable result. I will also talk about including a healthier nutrition and fitness plan into your life to help create your new, unshakable self. Here we go…

10: How Stress Makes Us Sick, Fat, Old, and Exhausted—And What to Do About It

You have heard the saying, "If you want something done, give it to a busy person." Whether it is their ability to multitask, to work at twice the normal speed, or to cram the most into every waking moment, busy people get things done. Unfortunately, they often pay a price for all that productivity in the form of chronic, unmanaged stress.

As if being busy wasn't enough, add to it a lack of sleep, a fitness routine that depletes instead of energizes, toxic relationships, a mindset that doesn't serve and inflammatory foods. Then mix in a few unresolved issues, stir in a life crisis, and you have the perfect recipe for stress-related symptoms, illnesses, conditions, and even disease.

Your body is magnificently wired to do all it can to protect you. When it senses anything stressful, it ignites the stress response. For example, let's say you are crossing the street and a car races toward you. Your mind recognizes this as a stressful situation, and the stress response in your body is immediately ignited. Cortisol, the stress hormone, and adrenaline are released. Blood and oxygen rush to your heart, lungs, and limbs so you can quickly and effectively jump the curb to safety. Your heart is pounding, you catch your breath, and thankfully, you are safe. Your body then quickly returns to its normal state.

This is the stress response working *for* you. It is designed to keep you safe, to keep you alive. With *chronic* stress, however, this same system is turned on and stays on, as if you are jumping the curb to safety 24/7. You can imagine how exhausting this can be over time.

Here is an example of the stress response being turned on from a normal experience you probably wouldn't suspect. Have you ever been in a rush and had to eat your lunch in a big hurry? You had no time, so you needed to quickly grab something before you left the house, left for a meeting—you get the idea. Remember that bloated and uncomfortable feeling you had? It makes sense to think you felt that way because you simply ate too quickly or swallowed too much air, but here is what really happened.

Your body, being as magnificent as it is, thought that when you ate your lunch in a hurry, you were in a crisis situation. Instead of blood and oxygen going to your digestive system to digest your food, your body decided, "This is a stress situation! Digest food? We have way more important things to do! We need to save her!" With that, your digestive system got shunted, it got completely shut down, and the blood and oxygen that would have gone to digest your food was instead diverted to your heart, lungs, and limbs so you could "jump the curb" and be safe. That is why you were left with that bloated and gassy feeling—and that was just lunch! Now imagine all of the stressors you have from the many roles you play within a given day—tasks, chores, errands, responsibilities, negative thoughts, unfinished projects, and unresolved issues. Your body is always trying to save you, and it is exhausting.

Many of the symptoms we walk around with, including illness and disease, are driven by chronic, unmanaged stress. These symptoms include fatigue, irritability, digestive issues, anxiety, depression, brain fog, hormonal issues, reduced libido, a suppressed immune system, and chronic illness.

We often see the symptoms of stress as normal, as a regular part of aging, something we just need to get used to. *But this isn't true.* Symptoms show up for a reason. They are your body's way of saying it needs your attention.

Take your car, for example. You know that red "check engine" light that comes on sometimes? It is your car's way of saying it needs your attention. Have you ever stuck a sticker over that red light so you didn't have to see it anymore? Of course not. But that is what we often do with our bodies. A symptom is your body's way of communicating with you, and if you mask it and neglect to see why the issue is presenting itself, the underlying cause can get worse; yet this is often the approach we take. If we can't sleep, we take a sleeping pill. If we need more energy, we look for an artificial boost from sugar or caffeine. If we are stressed, we take an antidepressant, alcohol, drugs, or food. The list goes on and on.

At the root of many of these symptoms is chronic, unmanaged stress. As we medicate and mask the symptoms, we do little to get to the root cause. Over time, the damage gets worse, the symptoms become more debilitating, and the fix usually becomes more expensive too. This is what happens when we ignore our symptoms, and this is *exactly* what happened to me during one of my many crashes.

I had a husband, home, four kids, and four dogs, and I was running a business with a full schedule of clients each day. I also had toxic relationships, way too much stress, emotional chaos, and I was trying to be everything to everyone, all the time. Symptoms such as extreme fatigue, weight gain, hair loss, skin problems, hormonal issues, brain fog, and back and neck pain started to show up. I was always sick with upper respiratory infections. I had the Epstein-Barr virus, bursitis, tendonitis, anxiety, and Hashimoto's thyroiditis. I also became insulin resistant and was pre-diabetic.

I also developed painful arthritis in my feet. From the outside, my feet looked fine, but X-rays showed that I had worn away the cartilage that cushions the joints. This made walking painful and wearing any kind of heels absolutely impossible. Every doctor I saw said the extensive damage was from years of running, but I wondered why it was that some people could run well into their later years, and here I was, in my forties and barely able to walk. It didn't make sense, but since I needed to get through my day, I started getting cortisone shots in both feet every three months just so I could manage the pain and be able to walk. My back was also in unbearable pain, and X-rays showed two herniated discs and degenerative disc disease. It was becoming unsafe for me to drive because I couldn't turn my head to look over my shoulder when changing lanes or getting on and off roads and exits. Doctors told me that it would only get worse as time went on and that surgery was my only option.

I didn't have the time (which really means that I didn't make the time) to take care of my health issues. I had kids to raise and a business to run, and taking time to figure out these symptoms and take care of myself was time I didn't have. Things got so bad that I eventually had to give up a thriving business with clients I loved. Here I was, a health expert, and I was anything but healthy. I was gaining weight and trying to teach people how to eat. I could barely walk, and I was trying to get people fit. I felt like a phony and a fraud. As a wife, I had no energy or desire to stay connected with my husband. I felt unattractive because my hair kept falling out, my skin was covered in acne, the weight kept piling on, my body hurt, and my stress consumed me. I was either filled with negativity and anxiety or felt flat and dull. All I wanted to do was sleep.

As a mom, I had no patience with my kids. I was so exhausted that I felt like I was walking through mud each day, yet I would sleep and feel as though I hadn't slept at all. I will never forget being on a call with someone who was interested in having me speak at their company. She needed to end our conversation because she was being called into a meeting. She said, "Debi, I'm so sorry, but I need to run. Let's pick up where we left off once my meeting is through. What's your number? I'll call you right back." I froze—I couldn't remember my own phone number! All I could think of to say was, "Can you hold on a minute?" I put her on hold and frantically searched through my cell for my own number, which I couldn't find. I got back on the call and said, "You know what? I'm not sure where I'll be in a few hours, so why don't I call you back?" She agreed, and as I hung up, I knew I had a real problem. I was spiraling into a state of anger, fear, hopelessness, and depression that seemed more and more difficult to escape.

Have you ever felt as though your health, life, and happiness were spinning out of control like mine were? My symptoms may have been different from yours, but it doesn't matter. What is important is whether they are preventing you from feeling good. Back to the story.

I finally decided to have surgery for the arthritis. Although it would mean being in a cast and on crutches for three months, it had to be better than living in constant and unrelenting pain. In making that decision, I had a lightbulb moment. I already knew about eating well and exercising, so I wondered if the toxic people in my life, the unbearable stress I was under, and the poisonous thoughts I was thinking were behind it all. (Perhaps in reading the previous chapters, you recognized this, too.)

With these questions in mind, and while I was healing from surgery, I decided to learn more about what relationships and stress can do to a person. I studied to become a Whole Health Coach, a health expert trained to teach how our lifestyles create either health and wellness or illness and disease. As I went through the program, my thoughts about what had been contributing to my illnesses and negative mindset were confirmed. Having nothing to lose, I did an experiment. Since I understood the healthy eating and exercise part of the equation, what would happen if I did something about the enormous amount of stress, the negative relationships, and the emotional upheaval they were causing?

The first thing I did was to cut the ties to my toxic relationships. Given that these were ties to my own family, it was extraordinarily painful, but there was such toxicity, so much negativity and pain, that it was a necessary first step for me. This step may not be right for everyone, but it was certainly right for me. Naturally, I questioned myself and anguished over my decision. I am so family-oriented and this decision went against many of my beliefs, but I saw so clearly the damage that holding on to those negative ties was doing to my health. It was also impacting my kids as they began to question what they were seeing and hearing.

Most people put their faith, trust, and belief into their closest relationships, and we assume, especially when we are young, that everything we are told is true and that we deserve the way we are being treated. We don't question it, and this can create a lifetime of pain. Once I dug deeper, I realized that my own programming and the baggage I hauled around because of it were massively impacting my health.

Once I cut those ties, I felt lighter, freer, and more at ease. This first step showed me how people can either help or hurt our health, mindset, and well-being. I was proving it in myself, and it fueled my motivation to take the next step.

Next, I cut back on my stress by learning to say no, delegate more, and stop caring about being judged. These changes were not easy at all, but they were crucial. They were painful and still can be today, so I understand how hard this may be for you. If this is what you need to do, though, start doing it, as it is vital for your health and well-being.

I also got rid of the superwoman cape, which had created an enormous amount of stress because of unrealistic expectations I placed on myself. I wasn't doing myself or anyone else a favor by trying to be so perfect. When I stayed true to my real priorities and let some of the rest go, I felt lighter and easier, and I experienced a new sense of freedom. These changes were working, and I kept healing. I want to be clear that changing and healing are rarely perfectly linear progressions. As one area improves, another may take a back seat for a while, and it is all okay. Done right, all areas eventually get the attention they need.

Finally, I addressed some of the stress-driven emotions that were constantly raging through me. I practiced being kinder and more compassionate with myself, and I spoke to myself the way I would speak to a friend. I realized I wouldn't have a friend in the world if I spoke to them as harshly and critically as I had been speaking to myself. As I changed my behaviors, my healing continued to improve. I eventually healed from each and every symptom and illness I had. I realized that you can eat well and exercise all day long, but if you neglect those other powerful areas of your life—your stress, your relationships, and your mental and emotional states—they will take you down. I was living proof.

My experiment put me on a path to healing and health that changed me both personally and professionally. Inspired by what I learned, I started writing books, speaking, and creating products and programs to share what I had learned with anyone who would benefit. I even became a Functional Diagnostic Nutritionist so I can test and treat people for stress-related issues. I was determined to get this new message of complete health out however I could so that I could help people heal. Without those negative influences in my life, my confidence, self-esteem, self-respect, and self-love dramatically improved. I started feeling much better, and I thrived at creating and managing my new business within my busy schedule. It all seemed to work—as long as I barely slept, never saw my friends, and continued to distract myself from some unresolved issues I wasn't ready to face. We even got two more dogs to add to the mix, and I juggled it all—once again—for a few more years.

Now, here is where I would love to tell you that everything was now perfect, that I lived happily ever after, having learned all the lessons I needed to learn forevermore. But that is not the case. Remember, growth is not always linear. Sometimes you take a few steps forward, have a setback, take a giant leap, another climb, a left turn, then a course correction—you get the idea.

As you might have guessed, a few years later, I crashed again. The good that came out of it, though, the best part, really, is that these different types of life crises have been the catalyst for this book and my new programs, which are designed to take what I have learned and use them to help you shorten your curve and prevent you from having to learn a lot of the lessons I learned by doing things the hard way. Remember when I said I used to believe that "good things don't come easy"? Many of the challenges I have faced I can swear were brought into my life because that belief was firmly in place.

So what do you do once you see what your stress is doing to you? For starters, see how your body is handling your stress. Is it showing itself in accelerated aging, weight gain, illness, or fatigue? Once you see how your stress is showing up, look at how you have been responding to it. Have you been masking your symptoms or alleviating them with a quick-fix approach? If so, it is not your fault. You were simply looking for relief, and "if you knew better, you'd do better." Now you know better.

Let's say you find that you have been masking stress-related symptoms with medications, food, and alcohol. With compassion and love, ask yourself what you really need. Is it downtime or support? Do you need to say no to something or delegate or cut back? Do you need something different or new that would take the stress down a notch? Do you need to lower your expectations a bit, not because you can't do something but because you love yourself enough to stop driving yourself into the ground? Could it be time to give up the need to be perfect and be okay with being perfectly imperfect? Remember, you write the rules, and you may have set up some unrealistic expectations for yourself.

If you are struggling with this, just think about what you would suggest to a friend. If they told you they were stressed, overwhelmed, exhausted, and unhappy, you would pour on the love and suggest they cut back, find help, and get support. You would help them realize they don't have to do it all. How about giving yourself your same brilliant advice? You are worth it. For your sake and for the sake of all within your care and reach, start being okay with being authentic, real, and powerfully you—even if it means your socks don't match, you don't do your own laundry, and you said you had plans when you secretly just wanted to binge-watch your favorite show. You are still incredible and I won't tell anyone our little secret.

11: Nutrition: Creating a Lean, Healthy Body

Working with thousands of women over the last twenty-five years, my motivation and intention for helping them get lean and healthy has drastically changed over time. In the past, my motivation may have been to help you look good in your skinny jeans, lose the baby weight, or get you ready for a special occasion. If that is what gets you going, great, but what I have found is that a lean and healthy body gives you so much more.

How will that energized body make you *feel*? How will it change how you *show up*? What will it allow you *to do*? How will it increase your confidence, improve your self-esteem, and power you through your day? In addition to making you look and feel good, cleaning up your diet can eliminate brain fog so that you think more clearly. It can reduce the likelihood of chronic illness, inflammation, weight gain, belly bloat, and conditions such as insulin resistance, type 2 diabetes, and obesity. While these incentives are certainly powerful, there is even more.

Powering up your body through healthy eating gives you an added layer of protection when you need it most. If you are hit with a life crisis, then having good health on your side as you go into the crisis provides additional strength, stamina, clarity, and confidence to help get you through what has been placed in your path. Getting ill when you are already otherwise healthy can help minimize the symptoms and duration, which, if you weren't healthy, would likely be much worse. Having good strength and stamina also makes healing easier should you undergo surgery.

Now consider a life crisis that knocks the confidence right out you. Take a situation such as divorce, for example. If you have gone through or are currently going through a divorce, your head may be reeling with all kinds of thoughts, beliefs, and behaviors resulting from your former partner's influence on you. Maybe they said hurtful and unkind things that caused you to believe you are not worthy, lovable, or beautiful. Maybe their actions have caused you to believe that somehow, you deserved that level of treatment, that you were lucky to even have such a partner. Perhaps your former partner sold you on the idea that all of the problems in the relationship were your fault, because they were unable to take responsibility for their actions. Now just imagine two scenarios when this storm hits.

One scenario is that the pain of the relationship had you self-soothe with food or alcohol. You couldn't think of a way to stop the hurt, stop the pain or stop feeling badly so quick relief through food or alcohol provided that temporary distraction and short term relief from your pain. Over time, it left you still feeling unhappy, and now feeling overweight and exhausted too. Now the reality of your crisis hits and not only is it time to pick up the pieces and rebuild your life but you feel so tired, so overwhelmed and so miserable with how your body looks and feels it seems like a bigger mountain to climb. See what I mean?

If this is where you are now, make peace with it and start the climb anyway. How? It starts with self-love. Remember, what you have been eating may not have been your priority, and that is okay. What matters is what you do *now*. Maybe in the past you treated your body poorly, only feeding it what was left over from your kids' plates, scraps you found in the cabinets, or whatever you could grab as you mindlessly raced from one activity to the next. Now consider that you deserve so much better. What would you feed yourself if you looked at yourself with love and kindness, with the understanding that while you may have been stuffing yourself to stuff the pain, you are now ready to heal?

This brings us to emotional eating, which is when we eat to soothe, calm, numb, and relax from our problems and our pain. With emotional eating, we are self-medicating. We try to flood ourselves with feel-good chemicals, and food is simply our drug of choice. If you have been medicating yourself with food, make peace with it. You were doing it because you wanted to feel better. Now, here is the real question to ask yourself: "What am I really hungry for?" Is it love, support, a need to relax, or a craving for something meaningful? Start feeding *that*, and it will be the beginning of the end of emotional eating.

It is also helpful to look at some of the other eating habits we have in place. When you look at them closely, you may find that some of your most unhealthy habits are there for a reason. Maybe eating that way keeps you connected to someone, since that is the "thing" you share with a partner. Maybe you automatically revert back to old behaviors when you are with certain members of your family. Maybe you eat comfort foods in search of the feeling you had when they were served to you long ago. Maybe you have a strong sugar addiction that you don't know how to get rid of, or maybe you just aren't ready to change. Whatever comes up, awareness is the first step. Once you see things clearly, take the next step to start feeding your body with love. Food and emotions are so intertwined that it is often hard to tell the difference, and there is a good chance you have been feeding yourself in an attempt to show yourself some love. Do you have a dysfunctional relationship with food? Is it a one-sided relationship where you love the cookies but they don't love you back? Start to untangle what you are eating and why. When you do, you will create that lean, healthy, strong body to match the strong mind, support system, and lifestyle we have been creating.

Please note that while I have plenty of programs and products to help in this area (such as my own line of <u>nutrition bars and shakes</u>), creating an eating plan for you, with specific foods to eat and what to steer clear of, is beyond the scope of this book. If you are interested in more information on how we can work together on an eating plan and more, please visit my website at www.PBTInstitute.com to learn about ways I can support you.

If you are still not sure about how to start eating healthier, here are a few things to consider. The first idea is that every single thing you do brings you in one of two directions: either further away or closer to the body, health, life, and lifestyle you want. If you do no more than make a decision to treat your body in a way that brings you toward what you want instead of away from it, you will find that your choices get healthier, and as they do, your body will respond with improved health, energy, and vitality.

Another idea is to check in with the ultimate version of you, the one you discovered in an earlier chapter. In order for her to look the way she did, she had to be eating healthier, right? Consult with her now. What does she fuel herself with? What changes did she make to create a body she feels good in? You have all the answers you need. They may be buried under a layer of pounds, but that is only temporary. The real you is one hot mama, and it is time to let her shine through. Finally, start eating a little cleaner to see how it feels. Treat your body a little bit better. Think: if you wouldn't give that food to a friend or your kids or anyone else you cared about, why would you give it to yourself?

A final note for this chapter: I have worked with many women whose excess weight provided some much needed protection, and here is how that works. Think about it. When we were young, we hid behind Mom's leg to feel safe. As we get older, that weight we now carry can serve the same purpose. As crazy as it sounds, you, too, may find that there is a benefit to the excess weight. Does it prevent intimacy that may be too frightening? Does it keep expectations at a certain (lower) level? Does it give you a reason to justify staying in a certain relationship, at a certain job, or does it prevent you from a particular experience? Only you know those answers, and if it is time to face them, it may help to get the support you need to dismantle those old beliefs, and free yourself from that old way of thinking. There is a beautiful woman under there, and it is time to create a body that matches your unshakable self.

12: Fitness: A Strong Body Equals a Strong Mind— And Looks Great, Too

I don't have to tell you all the benefits of exercise; you know there are many. Instead, I want you to think about how you want your body to look and feel. Of course you are going to look leaner, sleeker, and more toned with the right fitness plan, but the benefits are so much greater than that. When you are fit, you stand straighter, move better, walk with grace, and carry yourself with more confidence. When you are fit, you maintain your quality of life as things that may become challenging as we age (climbing stairs, carrying packages, even tying our shoes) remain easy. When you are already fit, you don't have to work twice as hard to overcome whatever physical challenges arise. When your life spins in areas that are out of your control, fitness can still be one of those areas that remain within your control. When you are slammed mentally and emotionally, you have one less hurdle to overcome as you bounce back.

Getting and keeping your body fit is an incredible way to de-stress, too, as you flood your body with healing endorphins and chemicals that just feel good. Being fit helps reduce depression, and through the rhythmic movement of cardio or your favorite yoga practice, you give your mind time to access subconscious thoughts, which helps you find solutions to unresolved issues. The benefits are endless. Becoming unshakable isn't complete without creating a body that is unshakable, too.

Being fit also sends out a message to others. When you are fit, you have certain qualities. You are dedicated, consistent, and persistent or you wouldn't look like that. Since how we are in one area of life is how we are in most areas, wouldn't having those qualities benefit you in other areas too? Think about it in business. Let's say a potential client, patient, customer, or company is considering working with you. You enter the room proudly, stand tall, carrying yourself in that elegant, confident way that fitness brings. Subconsciously, the person meeting with you can't miss the fact that you present the image of someone who loves themselves enough to take the time to be healthy. They see a picture of a woman radiating those positive qualities. That person may have been on the fence about working with you, but even though you have not yet spoken a word, they have received a subtle, positive message that your fit body helped to share.

Here is something else I know about fitness. If it is not a priority, it is one of the first things that will be bounced off your to-do list. We are masters at making up the perfect excuses for why we don't have time (which means we don't make time) for fitness. Having been in the field for over twenty-five years, I have heard them all. Of course, the lack of time is the biggest one, so let's take that one on first.

We often don't believe we have time for fitness because our plates are so filled with obligations and responsibilities we have piled on and we think taking time for fitness means neglecting something or someone else—and that would be selfish. So instead, we don't work out, we feel terrible, and somehow we believe that is better.

Taking care of your health is not selfish, it is *self-preservation*. If your goal is to be better for everyone within your care and reach, wouldn't a happier version of you be better for everyone? Right now and from this moment forward, please get rid of the idea that taking time for your fitness is selfish.

Next, our schedules are jam-packed, and we think working out would take way too long. We believe that working out has to be this long, laborious process in order for it to work. Well, we are all busy, and when we have demanding schedules, what we prioritize gets done. Are you watching too much TV, spending too much time on social media, or hitting the snooze button a few times? Look at where you can reclaim wasted time to create the body you want.

Now, I get it. I run a business, have four kids and six dogs, and am knee deep in a PhD program for Transpersonal Psychology. Fitness would never happen if I waited to find some free time. Do I need to get creative to ensure it gets done? Definitely. For example, while I love going to the gym, the travel time makes it too long of a process for me. Sure, I love the motivation and camaraderie, but my priority is to get it done. So my compromise is to go to the gym on the weekends when I have more time and get my fitness done at home during the week.

Your workout doesn't have to take up lots of time either. If you think you need an hour for a workout, I have some great news. We now know that burst training, HIIT (high intensity interval training) and short, intense interval training workouts transform your body in a fraction of the time. This means that the right interval program can blast fat and build muscle in the time it takes to drive to the gym.

Personally, I see how these workouts are creating a better result at fifty-plus years old than the workouts I did when I was in my twenties and before I had my kids.

Now let's take on the idea of getting motivated to work out. Another sigh of relief! You don't need to be motivated to work out, so please don't wait for it. In fact, you may never be motivated to get that workout in, so please don't wait for that day to come. Here is what I suggest instead. *Make it a habit.* A habit is something you just do. You don't even think about it, and you actually feel weird when you don't do it. You know you will feel good after a workout, and you know you will like the results. Instead of waiting for the motivation, create a habit so it gets done. How do you do that?

Here is one of my secrets. I have done this for years, and my clients from years ago still do it today. It really works. Don't be fooled by its simplicity. Ready? Before you go to sleep, lay out your fitness clothes and make a non-negotiable rule that you are not allowed to leave your bedroom until those fitness clothes are on. Why? With this little strategy, you give yourself a subconscious head start so that the first opportunity you have, you will get that workout in. Maybe you have to take out the dog, take care of the kids, or do your morning practice (a priority you learned about in Part 1), but, assuming you plan on working out in the morning, you will get your workout done at the first opportunity you have.

Here's the second reason. You may look at it as kind of deceptive but you are in on it so it is okay. You are throwing a little guilt at yourself here. Think about it. How bad will you feel if you haven't used your fitness clothes, and after doing all of your morning activities, you go back into your room and change out of them without getting that workout in? You will probably feel a little guilty. While this simple strategy gives you that subconscious head start and throws a bit of guilt your way, it works. Give it a try.

How do you start if you have put your fitness completely on hold? First, get clearance from your doctor to make sure it is okay to start a fitness program. Next, start moving according to your "fitness personality." This means finding what you like so you don't dread working out and will hopefully grow to enjoy it. Consider what would be a great first step for you. Is it getting outside and into nature or doing a hardcore weightlifting class or doing gentle yoga stretches? Would it help to work out with a buddy or have coaching from a personal trainer? Would you benefit from joining a gym?

Would working out from home with some basic equipment or streaming some great workouts right from your computer work better for you? Your options are endless.

As I mentioned about eating in the nutrition chapter, it is beyond the scope of this book to give you a detailed fitness program here. You can always get access to more tools and solutions at my website, www.PBTInstitute.com . For now, realize that part of your unshakable new self includes a healthy and fit body. The body you are creating is the vehicle you have to take you around to do all of the new and exciting things you plan to do. If your body is going to take you on a journey filled with new opportunities and exciting adventures, it needs to be up for the job. Let's get it ready to power you through whatever awaits.

13: Living an Unshakable Life

Look how far you have come! You didn't simply take in a few new ideas on your journey through this book, you created an *unshakable self*, built from the rubble of faulty thinking and living. This wasn't just growth, it was a complete transformation. To me, growth is a puppy growing into a dog. *Transformation is different.* Transformation is the caterpillar that makes the decision to go into a dark, lonely, and uncomfortable place. The caterpillar is willing to be deconstructed, emulsified, and unrecognizable from what it once was. It is willing to go through a messy, sticky, lonely, and challenging process. Because of that, it eventually emerges as one of the most magnificent creatures on the planet today: a butterfly. That is what has happened with you. You didn't simply learn a few new strategies, you entered the tunnel of transformation, perhaps sick, brokenhearted, and exhausted, and emerged with a new awareness and strategies to become unshakable and transformed.

When you picked up this book, the pain you felt because of your situation fueled your desire for something better, and I am sure you are already seeing proof of your transformation in the new way you now look, feel, and live. You did great but if you feel you want to dive in more deeply, I have created special programs designed to take you to the next level that you can find at www.PBTInstitute.com.

It is my hope that now that you know what it takes to be unshakable, you are able to let go of the excess baggage and pounds of pain and are able to see new opportunities, explore new possibilities, and invite a new direction into your life. While you may be experiencing enormous growth now that you are on the other side of your life crisis, you also know how to manage the painful triggers when they arise and see them with a keen awareness that helps you prevent a setback from ever derailing you again.

You have created a rock-solid foundation as a result of your effort, and while we may not know each other personally, please know that my heart is bursting with pride. You are my "she'ro." I am in awe of your strength, grit, resilience, and determination to bounce back. You are the people we read about, study, and learn from. You are the leader, the brave warrior who forges a path for others to follow. You are not only making a better life for yourself, you are demonstrating to others how to do the same. Nothing can take you down again—anything that tries to will be just another obstacle placed in front of you to show you how strong you really are. You've got this. You have been there and back, and now you have tools to help maintain your progress. You now have a powerful message of strength, resilience, healing, and love that you are ready to share with the world.

14: New Path and Next Steps

So, my unshakable friend, it is time to acknowledge the distance you have traveled so you can see just how incredible you are with your own two eyes. Remember that letter you wrote to yourself at the very beginning of this journey? That was a letter written to the version of you before all of the changes you have been making. It is time to read it again to see how far you have come. Please find that letter, read it with love and compassion, and we will pick up where we left off.

Go ahead. No reading any further until you find and read that letter. I am trusting you.

. . . waiting . . .

Okay, did you read it? I hope it fills your heart with love as you see that you did all you could with what you had available at the time. Reading the letter is an exercise in self-love, compassion, and grace. It should now clear why you created certain habits, why boundaries were crossed, and how unconscious living may have contributed to a crash. From a strong and more empowered place of wisdom and strength, seeing your own words to your former self will probably bring awareness, gratitude, and maybe even tears of joy.

Now that you are armed with ideas to help you physically, mentally, emotionally, psychologically, and spiritually, you will find yourself in a place very different from where you were before you started, so to wrap things up in a neat little bow, here is what I would like you to do now.

From this stronger, more evolved, healthier, and more healed place, please write another letter to yourself. This letter will clearly show you how far you have come. Write it to the version of you you have become and who you will continue to be. Write your goals, dreams, and visions of your future as you slowly and consistently pull them into your awareness and into your reality. Tell yourself how proud you are, how grateful you are for everyone who has crossed your path. Tell yourself how thankful you are for the lessons learned, for the insights, for the awareness, and for the growth. Let yourself know how loved, lovable, worthy, and deserving you are just because you are you. Finally, use this new awareness to create the boldest, most vibrant, colorful, enthusiastic, and courageous version of you that can exist.

There is so much more to you than what you have allowed yourself and the world to see. Unleash your brilliance, my friend.

You have been given an opportunity to create an impact and a legacy you may not have believed in before, and it is my greatest hope that you believe it now.

Thank you for your time, your willingness to grow, and your contribution to everyone you touch. You have touched my heart, and I can only imagine the lives you will impact as you continue moving forward.

So, with another virtual hug, please stay in touch. Email me at Debi@PBTInstitute.com to share your story of transformation, the changes you have made, and how your life has changed because of your life crisis, your self-induced life crisis, or your midlife crisis. Come to one of my talks so I can meet you in person. (You can keep up with my new programs, where I will be speaking, and get my special ebook and more by heading over to www.PBTInstitute.com .) Most of all, thank you for the opportunity to support you in this part of your life. My greatest wish for you is that you continue to become and stay *UNSHAKABLE*.

With love and deepest respect,

Dr. Debi

ABOUT THE AUTHOR

Dr. Debi Silber, President of The Silber Center for Personal Growth and Healing/The PBT Institute in New York and founder of www.PBTInstitute.com, is a transformational psychologist, a recognized health, mindset, empowerment, and personal development expert. She is a Transpersonal Psychologist, a Registered Dietitian with a Master's degree in nutrition, a certified personal trainer, and a Whole Health Coach™. She has two certifications in pre- and post-natal fitness, and is a Functional Diagnostic Nutritionist. She is also a working mom with four kids and six dogs and has been married to her husband, Adam, for over twenty-seven years.

Debi gets it. She understands the unique demands of the busy professional because she is one. From being president of her company, managing a big family, and going through a PhD program, Debi knows what it takes to get results without wasting time.

Everything she teaches comes from that perspective: results without fluff. Whether she is teaching audiences, writing for popular websites, or working with her private clients, Debi's energy, unique style, strategies, tools, and methodology have become the secret edge to some of the healthiest, most dynamic, and successful people today.

Debi is a sought-after speaker and the author of three books recommended by Jack Canfield, Brian Tracy, Marshall Goldsmith, and others. She has contributed to *The Dr. Oz show*, *FOX*, *CBS*, *TEDx*, *The Huffington Post*, *Forbes*, *Shape*, *Self*, *WebMd*, *Working Mother*, *Glamour*, *Ladies Home Journal*, *Women's World*, *MSN*, and *YahooShine*, to name a few, and is the creator of of deliciously healthy nutrition bars and shakes designed to curb cravings and crush sugar addictions.

Between her talks, online private and group coaching, and in-person coaching, Debi has led thousands of people to heal physically, mentally, emotionally, psychologically and spiritually from a life crisis. Because of her diverse credentials, experience, and motivational style, Debi takes her audiences right through their comfort zones to where their best lives begin.

Debi has achieved such honors as HealthTap's 2015 Nutrition Industry winner, a 2014 Top Ranked US Executive by the National Council of American Executives, and is a Notable American Woman. She has been featured as a self-improvement expert in books including *Power Moms: The New Rules for Engaging Mom Influencers Who Drive Brand Choice* (Maria Bailey; 2011) and was profiled in the textbook, *Exploring Global Issues: Social, Economic, and Environmental Interconnections* (Henderson, Shaw, Skelton, and Jacob; 2013), which aims to inspire students to pursue similar careers.

Debi offers speaking, high-level private and group coaching, as well as online programs for those who want immediate action through videos, tools, strategies, coaching, live Q&A calls, and support. All of her programs are designed to inspire, empower, and transform.

Dr. Debi Silber

Find out more at www.PBTInstitute.com

To watch Debi's popular TEDx talk:

https://www.youtube.com/watch?v=XX30i6nC7ro

To connect with Debi:

Twitter: https://twitter.com/DebiSilber

Facebook: https://www.facebook.com/InspireEmpowerTransform

LinkedIn: https://www.linkedin.com/in/debisilber

CAN I ASK YOU A FAVOR?

If you enjoyed this book and found it useful, I would really appreciate it if you would post a short review on Amazon. I read all the reviews personally so that I can continually write what people want. I appreciate it, and I appreciate you!

Made in the USA
Las Vegas, NV
07 April 2021